PITCH POND CURSE

Kathryn White
Illustrated by Alan Clarke

Chapter 1
The Curse of Jack Ridley

On 13 October, 1848, Jack Ridley stole in the village of Holbury for the last time. Jack crept into Mr Hamley's cottage and snatched the old man's bread money from the bench. Mr Hamley saw the torn breeches and bright orange hair, so he knew Jack was the culprit.

Everyone in Holbury said Jack was cursed because his mother died whilst giving birth to him. So Jack stole and, when he was caught, his father, Sam Ridley, beat him.

Mr Hamley told everyone about his stolen money and soon the news of Jack's treachery reached Sam Ridley. Sam was now sitting outside his cottage, waiting for Jack. It was Jack's twelfth birthday, but the only gift he would be getting would be a lashing.

Behind the Ridley cottage, on the far side of Folly Wood, was a pond so deep it was said to be the dwelling of an evil water spirit. Pitch Pond stood as black and still as death itself.

No one ventured to Pitch Pond. Not, that is, until 13 October, 1848.

On that day, Jack rounded the corner to his cottage and a hand grabbed his hair.

"Steal, will you? I'll strap you blue," boomed his father, Sam.

Jack fell, crashing onto a log pile. The logs rolled and tumbled out from under him.

"Vermin. Trouble since you was born!" Sam yelled, as he raised his belt.

"Wasn't me, Da. Wasn't!" Jack hollered.

"Lying rat," hissed Sam.

Jack looked up at his father and something snapped deep inside him. Instead of fear, Jack suddenly felt raging fury for all the lashings he had been given since he was young.

"I hate you!" Jack shouted viciously at Sam.

Shocked, Sam stepped back. But his boot caught on a fallen log and he stumbled, crashing into the cottage wall.

Jack stood up, rigid; his breathing was quick and shallow. He went over to where Sam lay, motionless. "Da? Can you hear me?" he whispered. He knelt beside his father. "You cursed me, Da. Now I curse you and all the village," Jack whispered coldly. "I curse you all."

Sam groaned and Jack leapt to his feet. Looking round quickly, he ran off into Folly Wood.

Ravens circled in the bleak sky as Jack slowed to a brisk walk through the trees and sang a strange little ditty to himself. "Jack be quick, Jack be bold. Jack's accursed soul be sold."

Jack felt a strange power invisibly drawing him to Pitch Pond. He had never ventured this far into the wood before, but for some reason, he now felt strong enough to face anything. "Jack Ridley is invincible," he called out. He threw back his head, wild with laughter.

The closer he got to Pitch Pond, the quieter the woodland became; in time, there was no birdsong, no rustling of leaves. A yellow mist drifted in patches across the soggy ground. The mist reached out, touching the tips of Jack's boots.

Jack sniffed the air. It smelt rotten, reminding him of the odd carcass of rabbit he'd sometimes stumbled upon near his cottage.

He took a stolen coin from his pocket and held it glinting in the strange light. A chill wind swept over him and then – whoosh, a shadow snatched the coin from his fingers.

"Oi!" Jack shouted, startled.

The coin twinkled in the sharp claws of a raven as it flew on towards Pitch Pond.

"I'll hang you and pluck you dead!" Jack yelled, chasing the raven through the mist. "Only Jack Ridley steals," he hissed darkly.

Jack crashed through trees and thorns and found himself standing right on the very edge of Pitch Pond. A white moon shone brightly, illuminating the bare silhouettes of the trees. They looked transformed, dancing in grotesque shapes beneath the evening sky.

Jack blinked. Through the mist, he thought he saw goblins; their red eyes peering out of the darkness. The skin prickled on the back of his neck. "Jack's not afraid," he called softly.

He looked at the still water of the pond. There was no reflection of moon or trees on its surface. Only blackness stared back at him.

Then, a sharp finger prodded his back. Jack swung round, but no one was there. Jack then saw the raven, perched on a branch, playing teasingly with the coin. "Give it back," he called.

He grabbed another coin from his pocket and placed it by his feet. "Come and get it," Jack snarled.

The raven swooped like lightning and flew out above the centre of the pond. It shrieked, and the coin fell from its beak into the water.

"Thief!" shouted Jack angrily.

Pitch Pond began to glug and bubble noisily. Jack watched, petrified, as the raven began to transform in the yellow mist. Its head disintegrated into thick, black vapours, swirling and whirling into strange demonic faces. The evil spirit let out a shrill scream that echoed across the woodland.

Jack's stomach retched in terror as tentacles grew out from the spirit's body. Their clawed hands beckoned Jack to enter the pond.

Jack stumbled back in horror. He turned to run, but the trees closed into a twisted gnarled wall.

The spirit spoke; its voice reverberated like thunder through Jack's body. "You dare to challenge the spirit of darkness? You dare to demand the return of the coin?"

Every ounce of Jack's new courage seeped out of him. "You can keep the coin," he cried.

"'Tis not the coin I shall keep," said the evil spirit. Its tentacles darted across the pond's bubbling surface, their claws wrapping tightly, painfully around Jack's ankle. "I have been waiting for you," said the spirit darkly. It yanked Jack off his feet, tugging him down into the soft wormy clay.

Jack dug his fingers into the mud, desperate to resist the pull of the spirit. "No!" Jack yelled as he was dragged inch by inch into Pitch Pond.

As Jack sank, he raised his chin up, gasping. He caught a last glimpse of the beautiful white moon above him before disappearing into the watery depths.

Jack Ridley came face to face with the black spirit. They tumbled together in the darkness, the spirit squeezing the life from Jack. But, as Jack gave out his last breath, he saw in his mind's eye the new life that had been planned for him.

Chapter 2
Possession

Ryan woke with a start.

He looked at the clock by his bed. "Crud, late," he mumbled irritably. Ryan could hear the steady flow of traffic heading into Highbury town centre.

He leapt out of bed, threw on his crumpled school clothes and thundered downstairs.

"Nat?" he called.

No answer. Natalie, his sister, had already left for school and their mum had gone to work. Ryan spotted Natalie's left-over cereal and dregs of milk in the bowl. He grabbed the bowl, gulped down the contents, then wiped his mouth with the tea towel and hurried out of the door.

It was grey outside. Ryan's breath misted in the air. "This sucks," he said.

Ryan was late and already on a warning

from Miss Thomson. But there was late and there was early-late. If he was early-late, then he could come up with a plausible excuse.

Ryan headed off the busy road, opting for a short cut across country. He leapt over a fence, breaking into a run across a field.

Fifteen minutes until registration. Why hadn't Natalie woken him? He knew she would have done; but he would have just turned over and gone back to sleep.

After a while, Ryan stopped. He was lost again. Every time he took short cuts, he got lost. "Ah, skits," he cursed. The hum of traffic was now barely audible.

Ryan carried on and soon reached a small area of woodland. He remembered seeing a wood behind the trading estate near school. He hurried through the trees and suddenly found himself at the edge of a circular glade. At its centre was a massive indent in the ground.

Ryan shivered. It looked as if the coming winter had already killed off any life that attempted to exist here.

As Ryan walked across the glade, the ground became soggy under-foot, squelching beneath his trainers. When he reached the centre, his trainers sank down into thick, black liquid. "Ah, man!" Ryan said, lifting each foot and seeing his black, wet socks.

Ryan took long jumps across the mud, trying to limit the damage to his trainers. When he reached the far side, even his trousers were sopping wet.

Hassled, Ryan raced on, but suddenly felt a sharp pain in his foot. Something had slipped down the inside of his trainer and was pressing against his skin. Peeling off his sodden sock, he found a hard, round object. He cleaned it on the inside of his blazer and smiled. "Cool," he said, inspecting the old coin. "Could be valuable." He put the coin into his blazer pocket, put his trainer back on and hurried through the wood.

He was just coming out of the wood when he saw someone leaning against a tree. As Ryan drew closer, the figure stepped out and blocked his path.

"You've got something that belongs to me," hissed the stranger angrily.

Ryan was shocked. The stranger – a boy – had bright orange hair and was wearing what looked like torn skater shorts to his knees and a pair of retro boots. He stared coldly at Ryan with piercing eyes.

Ryan guessed the boy had skipped off school, but he had no time for this jerk and his stupid games. "No I haven't," he said impatiently.

"Return the coin to me here and now, and you will be free forever. But if you leave with it, you can never go back to your normal life," said the boy, holding out his hand.

Ryan looked at the boy as if he were crazy.

Ryan knew that if he admitted to having the coin, he'd have to give up a possible priceless treasure, and anyway, he was now wet, uncomfortable, angry and late.

Ryan decided – finders keepers. "Listen, I don't know what coin you're talking about. So leave me alone," he said quickly.

The boy looked intently at Ryan. "Your soul is the price of the coin," he stressed calmly.

What a joker! Ryan thought smugly to himself. He decided to end the conversation quickly. "Sure! Now out of my way," he demanded.

The boy suddenly grinned; his eyes seemed to flash with delight as he stepped aside.

As Ryan left the wood, the boy called darkly after him, "Then I'll be seeing you again."

Ryan glanced over his shoulder. "Yeah, right!" he scoffed.

Chapter 3
The Truth and Nothing but the Truth

Ryan squelched into class an hour late and feeling dreadful.

Miss Thomson was angry. Not only was Ryan late, but he was covered in mud and making a mess of the classroom floor. The class laughed and hooted with delight.

"I hope you've got a good explanation for turning up late in this condition," snapped Miss Thomson.

"Aliens snatched his bag again, Miss?" shouted Alex Redman.

"Nah, he's been wrestling the mighty mud monster," sniggered Shane Lewis.

"Enough of the smart comments, thank you. It's a pity you don't use your over-active imaginations more often in English lessons. Then we'd see better school reports," said Miss Thomson.

All eyes rested on Ryan. He desperately tried to think of one of his clever excuses, but nothing came. "Miss, I got lost, fell into a bog and found an ancient coin," he blurted.

The class erupted into laughter again. A hint of a smile drew across Miss Thomson's lips.

"Don't leave the bog seat up next time!" shouted Alex Redman.

"Well, you've had quite a morning, Ryan!" said Miss Thomson calmly.

"Honest, Miss. It's true." Ryan padded up to her desk, leaving a trail of mud behind him. He fumbled in his blazer pocket for the old coin.

It had gone.

"Well?" Miss Thomson looked dubiously at Ryan. "Where's your treasure?"

Ryan groped in all of his pockets. They were empty. "I don't believe it, Miss. It's gone!" Ryan said in disbelief.

Miss Thomson sighed wearily.

"Nice one, Ryan," called Shane Lewis sarcastically.

Ryan swung round. "Shut it, Shane, or I'll shut you," he said, clenching his fists.

"You and the mud monster," laughed Shane.

"Right, that's enough everyone!" snapped Miss Thomson. "You'd better go and get changed into your PE kit," she said, turning to Ryan. "Oh, and Ryan," she whispered to him, "what did I tell you happened to Pinocchio?"

Defeated, Ryan shrugged and replied, "He never passed his exams, and couldn't afford his nose job, Miss."

Miss Thomson frowned as Ryan plodded out. Although she had to admit that the lies he told in class showed great imagination, she was also aware that Ryan was fast becoming the butt of everyone's jokes.

"What do you want for your birthday?" Natalie asked, munching her tea.

"Your Mindblowers CD," Ryan said quickly.

"Okay, I'll buy it for you. Then you won't

keep taking mine," she said wisely.

Ryan had almost forgotten that his birthday was looming – Tuesday 13 October.

He spent the night planning his wish-list of presents, then fell into a deep sleep.

In the middle of the night, Ryan was woken by a loud knocking noise. He sat bolt upright and rubbed his eyes. "What is it, Nat?"

There was no answer.

Ryan lay down again, but jumped when another loud noise echoed around his bedroom. He switched on the bedside lamp.

"Mum?" he called.

He hopped out of bed and opened the bedroom door.

Nothing.

As soon as he closed the door, the noise came again. Ryan now realised it was something hitting the outside of his bedroom window. Sleepily he plodded across and opened the window wide.

25

"Remember me?" came a voice from the garden.

Ryan looked down onto the lawn. Rubbing his eyes, he was shocked to see the strange, orange-haired boy he'd seen in the wood.

Ryan thought his tired eyes were playing tricks on him, because the boy's image seemed to be weaving like smoke in the darkness.

"I told you we would meet again," called the boy. "You lied to me about the coin. You did have it. Now we will have to seal a bargain."

Ryan was rattled and fed up. He wanted to be rid of this annoying nuisance once and for all. "Get lost," he shouted.

"Only when you return the coin," said the boy, his voice smoking up from somewhere below.

"I haven't got your stupid coin, moron!" Ryan shouted angrily.

Suddenly, the boy shot up into the air, heading straight towards Ryan's bedroom window.

Terrified, Ryan slammed the window shut just as the boy reached the glass. The boy hovered outside, shifting and moving like smoke.

Ryan stumbled back onto the floor in horror, but couldn't drag his eyes away from the terrifying vision. The boy floated outside, looking through the glass. He was watching Ryan's terror with delight.

"Jack Ridley has waited 150 years for this. This is the bargain we'll make. You must bring the coin back to where you found it – Pitch Pond." The words came in whispers, as if the boy were right beside Ryan, rather than floating outside the window. "Bring the coin on 13 October. You can give it to me, as my birthday present," said the boy darkly.

Ryan felt as if his heart would pound out of his chest. He closed his eyes, praying it was just a nightmare, desperate that when he next opened them the horrific spectre would be gone. Slowly he opened his eyes and tried to see beyond the reflections on the glass.

The window was clear, all but for the stars and moon.

Ryan sighed, relieved. Then he screamed in shock as an ice-cold hand rested on his shoulder. He slowly turned his head to see the boy who called himself 'Jack Ridley' kneeling only centimetres from his face.

There was an overpowering smell. It was the same smell that Ryan had tried removing from his trainers after he'd marched through the muddy glade.

Jack spoke, and his breath cut like ice across Ryan's warm cheek. "I told you the price of the coin. Soon you will pay with your soul."

Chapter 4
The Dark Decision

"Ryan? Are you okay in there?" Natalie called through the door.

Ryan was dumb. He daren't move, but watched petrified as the spirit of Jack Ridley disappeared, leaving a pungent vapour.

Natalie marched in. "Ryan, it stinks in here," she complained.

Ryan was sitting on the floor shaking. Natalie walked up to him and put her hand on his shoulder. Ryan leapt into the air, yelling in terror.

"Hey, it's me, dumbo. Your sister, remember?" Natalie said, amused and surprised. "Were you having a nightmare?"

"No!" protested Ryan. "Nat, please, you've got to help me. I've just seen a ghost. It says it's going to steal my soul, Nat. It's going to take it!"

Natalie looked daggers. "Not another one of your alien tales, Ryan Webb?"

"Please, Nat! I ... I think I'm going to ... " Ryan stuttered, terrified and unable to finish his sentence.

"Ryan, how many times have you got me into trouble with your lying? How much have you upset Mum with your lying? Well, nobody has the time for it tonight, loser," Natalie snapped, and stormed out.

For the rest of the night, Ryan sat up in bed. Rigid with fear, he peered out into the moonlight, waiting for the return of the ghost of Jack Ridley. Hour after hour his mind twisted and turned in circles. By dawn he had come to a decision. If he ever wanted to be free of the evil ghost of Jack Ridley, there was only one thing to do. Find the coin and return it to the boy, as he had been told to do.

Miss Thomson handed out photocopied maps. "This is Holbury. Does anyone know where Holbury is?" she asked.

Alison Jay's hand shot up in the air.

Miss Thomson nodded.

"It's here, Miss. We live in Holbury," Alison said quickly.

"It's Highbury, dumbo!" Shane Lewis piped up from the back of the class.

"Actually Shane, Alison is correct. This is Holbury. The town name changed about a hundred years ago to Highbury and there have been quite a few other changes too. What I want everyone to do is to take a photocopied map of old Holbury, and compare it to the new map of Highbury. You'll find the new map in the town library. Then list as many changes as you can," Miss Thomson instructed.

The bell rang for break and everyone bolted out of the door. Everyone except Ryan Webb; he'd fallen asleep over his desk. Normally Miss Thomson would have given Ryan a grinding for it, but today she was concerned about him.

When he wasn't turning up for school covered in mud with wild stories about treasure, he was dragging himself in looking terrified and half dead. She decided it was time for a talk.

She shook Ryan gently. He leapt off his seat and howled in fright. Miss Thomson jumped back surprised. "Ryan, are you all right?" she asked.

Ryan rubbed his face, trying to focus in the harsh classroom light.

"Sorry. I haven't had any sleep," he said.

"What's the problem?" said Miss Thomson.

"You wouldn't believe me if I told you, Miss. Nobody ever does," Ryan said, staring blankly at the floor.

"Probably not, Ryan, but why don't you try anyway?" she prompted.

Ryan sat down, looked at Miss Thomson and said calmly, "I've lost my soul, Miss."

For the first time in fifteen years of teaching, Miss Thomson was lost for words. "Pardon me?" she replied after a while.

"Somebody's got my soul and I need to get it back." Ryan said it as if he were talking about a CD or a new computer game.

"Ryan, people can't take souls," she said patiently.

"Jack Ridley can," said Ryan, his eyes clouding with tears.

"Ryan, what on earth are you talking about?" Miss Thomson said quickly.

"See? I knew you wouldn't believe me. I knew it," said Ryan. "But it's true. A ghost appeared last night. He said I have something that belongs to him. A coin. I found it in the glade he calls Pitch Pond. But ... but it's not a pond any more. It's just black mud. I didn't pick it up. I didn't steal it like that. It fell into my shoe. I ... I just lied about finding it, that's all. He's been dead for 150 years; he told me so last night."

Miss Thomson remained composed. "Ryan, this has to stop now. Or people will never take you seriously and that's a terrible burden to live with," she said sympathetically.

"Don't worry, Miss. I don't think I'll be living for long anyway," said Ryan hopelessly.

"Ryan, you really are a character," chuckled Miss Thomson. She pushed the copy of the old map of Holbury nearer to Ryan. "So where do you think your Jack Ridley lived 150 years ago?"

Ryan looked at the map for a few moments and then pointed decisively to the area marked 'Folly Wood'. "It must be there, in that wood. Just in the centre is a place called Pitch Pond, Miss. Only it isn't a pond any more – it's just black mud. That's where I found the coin."

"I see," said Miss Thomson, surprised by Ryan's decisive answer.

"When I walked through the wood, it wasn't as big as it is on this map. I think the trading estate's where some of it was and ..." Ryan stopped and stared at the map. "I have to go back. I have to return the coin."

"I'm sure when you find your mysterious coin, you'll return it. But Ryan, do calm down," said Miss Thomson.

Ryan sighed, "Okay, Miss."

As Ryan left, Miss Thomson felt a pang of sadness. She wondered if he would ever tire of making up his wild stories.

Chapter 5
Discovery

Ryan hadn't slept properly all week. When he did crash out from exhaustion, his mind was full of the terrors of Jack Ridley's visit.

Every day, Ryan searched high and low for the old coin. He went through every pocket again and again. It would be his birthday on Tuesday, and he was desperate to find the coin and return it to the glade before the end of the weekend. Then he pledged to himself to make a fresh start in his life and never, ever lie again. He now wanted people to believe what he said!

Natalie was still huffy with him for talking rubbish again. His mum had started shovelling spoonfuls of vitamins into him, saying he was coming down with something. Even TV programmes and computer games seemed a million miles away from the dark world he now found himself in.

After lunch on Sunday, Ryan fell asleep. When he woke up it was dusk. Ryan's heart jolted with panic. He looked at the clock – it was only four o'clock, so he still had time to find the coin. Knowing he had school in the morning, he had one last chance to find it and he knew there was only one place it could be. He must have dropped it at the edge of the wood where he had first met Jack Ridley's ghost.

Shakily, he put on two layers of jumpers, his wellies, and grabbed the torch. He darted outside and headed towards the field.

Ryan found the glade quickly, almost as if something had instinctively guided him to it. Instead of crossing the centre of the glade he hurried around the edge, being careful not to step on the inner, marshy ground.

Something swooped across the glade, its black outline moving with lightning speed.

Ryan saw the approaching shadow and ran for the cover of the trees. His heavy wellies made it hard for him to gain any speed. Then he felt something touch the top of his head; it felt like the flick of a hand.

41

Ryan looked up, breathless and trembling, but was relieved to see it was only a bird; a large raven had just landed on a branch ahead of him.

Ryan hurried on. The raven's eyes flashed yellow in the half-light as it hissed at him. When Ryan came out of the trees on the far side of the glade, he breathed in deeply. He felt as if he had been walking in a black, airless tunnel and had only just emerged into fresh, clean air.

He decided that after finding the coin he would return home the long way round, through the busy estates and roads. He flicked on the torch and shone it onto the moist grass. As he searched, he kept an eye on the afternoon sky and decided he had ten minutes until dark and no more.

Ryan became more and more frustrated. He dropped onto his hands and knees in the wet grass, pulling it back almost blade by blade. The raven had perched above and was watching him. It cackled and screeched at him with delight.

Frantic, Ryan kept searching, his sharp blue eyes looking for the tiniest glint of silver. Then he saw something shining no more than a metre away. His heart leapt.

He reached out for it in the long grass. Yes, it was the old coin. He'd found it. He would be saved.

Just as he was about to pick it up, a hand shot down onto the coin.

Ryan screamed. He turned his head and saw the ghostly image of Jack Ridley crouching beside him.

Jack's claw-like fingers had wrapped themselves around the old coin. His lips broke into a broad grin. "What have we here? A thief is it?" Jack whispered, tormenting Ryan.

Ryan's heart pounded and his stomach heaved.

"It's the coin. I found it first. It's mine, but I was going to return it to you," Ryan said desperately.

"So it is a coin," said Jack, amused. "What say you?" Jack asked of the raven perched above them.

The raven hissed and screeched. Ryan covered his ears against the high-pitched noise.

Jack leaned closer to Ryan. "Take the coin," said Jack with contempt. "But you know the bargain. You must return it to me in two days – on 13 October."

Ryan reached out and clasped the coin tightly in his palm.

"I shall be seeing you soon." Jack's voice echoed around him as he disappeared.

Ryan watched the raven alight and fly away. He stayed hunched in the wet grass, shocked and silent. Suddenly, he realised he had the precious coin in his hand. He clasped it tight in his palm and put it to his lips as if praying. "I'll come back," he whispered desperately. "I'll come back and be free."

Chapter 6
The Myth

Miss Thomson smiled with delight at the pile of research papers Alison Jay placed on her desk on Monday morning. "Well," said Miss Thomson, "somebody's taken the project seriously."

Ryan sidled in and flopped down into his seat. Miss Thomson looked around the room. Everyone had a small pile of papers, photos, news clippings and information; everyone except Ryan Webb and Shane Lewis.

"Shane, where's your research?" Miss Thomson asked, already knowing what reply to expect.

"I was sick, Miss. End of last week. My mum's written me a note." Shane dug into his pocket and pulled out a scrunched-up piece of paper. He held it out to Miss Thomson.

"I don't think I'm going to read it, Shane.

I'll just speak to your mother instead."

Shane groaned and put his head in his hands.

Ryan only had one piece of paper. Miss Thomson looked anxiously towards him. "Ryan? What about you?" she said.

"It's all here, Miss," said Ryan, holding up the photocopied map she'd initially given out to the class. It was covered in Ryan's handwritten notes. "It's got all the changes listed, Miss," said Ryan.

"Oh, I see. And where did you get the information from?" Miss Thomson said sceptically, seeing Ryan had no research papers.

"My head, Miss. Like I remembered where everything was 150 years ago. Just my head. It's weird, I can't explain it. It all just came to me. The wood, Pitch Pond, Jack Ridley's cottage, Mr Hamley's place, everything."

The class erupted into guffaws of laughter.

Miss Thomson looked at Ryan with concern. He was still keeping to his ridiculous tale of ghosts, lost souls and the evil Jack Ridley. She decided to ignore his story-telling, and hoped that he would realise how foolish he was going to look when everyone's work was marked. "I'll go through your work tonight, Ryan," sighed Miss Thomson.

That night, Ryan carefully placed the old coin in his shoe and tucked it under his bed. He'd be sure to remember it then.

Tomorrow would be 13 October, his birthday. But he had only one thought before he fell asleep; the return of the coin and his freedom. He knew he would go back to the glade, face Jack Ridley and give him what he wanted.

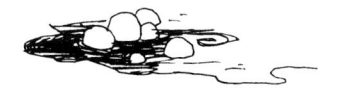

Miss Thomson sat at home surrounded by project papers. She'd already discovered much about Highbury, or Holbury, that she never knew, and was very pleased with the input of most of her pupils.

Alison Jay had submitted particularly excellent homework. She had even turned up a document noting the last recorded murder in Holbury.

It was a man by the name of Sam Ridley. Sam had been accused of murdering his son, Jack, on 13 October, 1854, after Jack disappeared. Because the boy was his son, Sam had been spared a public hanging, but he had been sent to prison.

Miss Thomson was about to place the paper onto the marked pile when something caught her attention. It was a name. It was Jack Ridley.

Miss Thomson snatched up Ryan's map. Her heart skipped a beat. Ryan had clearly outlined cottages and listed the names of their owners. Miss Thomson felt a chill as her eyes rested on the Ridley cottage. Just behind the cottage, Ryan had mapped out an area called Pitch Pond in the centre of the woodland. He had drawn an arrow pointing to its centre and written the words 'Jack Ridley'.

The more Miss Thomson studied Ryan's

map, the more she realised how much of his information matched the historical papers that the rest of the class had submitted. Miss Thomson realised too that everything Ryan had said that day in class was true. When he had arrived in class without research papers, everyone had laughed at him. Yet Ryan had stayed calm, and was able to state every last historical detail about Holbury.

Miss Thomson shivered as she also realised that when Ryan had first told her about Jack Ridley and the date of his death, he would have had no previous knowledge of her project. So how could he have foretold the research for it? Something was wrong. It didn't add up. The names Ryan had listed on the cottages; the bakery, the blacksmiths, the old inn – he had given so much more historical information than anyone else in class. It would normally have taken someone weeks to come up with Ryan's findings.

Miss Thomson picked up Alison Jay's report again. She read that Sam Ridley had been accused of drowning his son Jack in Pitch Pond. It was noted that a search of the pond had never been done because the local police refused to go there. The reason for this was that locals believed the pond was cursed by an evil black spirit; a spirit that would steal the souls of its victims.

Miss Thomson clenched the papers tightly in her hand. Panic and fear swept over her as she remembered Ryan looking up at her and his despairing words, "I've lost my soul, Miss."

She closed her eyes in disbelief. Something evil had happened, something beyond her imagination and wisdom. Miss Thomson looked out into the night. She knew that Ryan Webb was telling the truth. She knew that he was in great danger.

Chapter 7
Paying the Price

On Tuesday 13 October, Miss Thomson sat watching anxiously out of the classroom window. She was waiting for one last student. She had taken the register. Everyone was present except Ryan.

Because it was Ryan's birthday, she frantically hoped that Ryan would arrive at school late as he had often done before. But by ten o'clock, Miss Thomson's concern had grown. She tried to phone Ryan, but there was no answer. By lunchtime, she decided to call in at his home.

She headed down to the headteacher's office, arranged cover for her class, and raced out of the school. As she approached Ryan's house she knew no one was in. The house stood empty and dark. She knocked, not expecting an answer.

After a while Miss Thomson knew where she would find Ryan. Grasping Ryan's map, she made her way towards the trading estate behind the school, and to the woodland surrounding Pitch Pond.

Miss Thomson noticed that the sky above the wood had turned scarlet as if the midday light was instantly turning to dusk. As she came closer to the wood she saw a black cloud of ravens, circling silently in the sky.

She stepped into the darkness of the trees. Instinctively she wanted to leave. She wanted to return to the safe familiar site of the school, but she pledged to herself that she would not return without Ryan.

The air felt cold and a chill breeze stung her eyes. She looked back. Now there were only trees.

There was no sign of civilisation at all.

Suddenly she glimpsed out of the corner of her eye the figure of a boy walking through the trees ahead. Miss Thomson quickened her pace, to catch up with him. "Ryan, stop. Wait," she called urgently.

The boy ignored her and hurried on in his tracks. Miss Thomson then realised it wasn't Ryan. The boy was about the same age as Ryan, but he had bright orange hair and was dressed in strange clothes. He disappeared amongst the trees.

Moments later, Miss Thomson emerged at the edge of the glade. She knew immediately that the sunken, muddy centre had once been some kind of water-logged area. She guessed that she had found Ryan's evil Pitch Pond.

Miss Thomson looked over to the far side of the glade and froze. There was Ryan. He had stepped out from the trees and was moving slowly towards the very centre of the glade.

She watched in terror as black, bubbling liquid began to rise from the grassy earth. As Ryan neared the pond's centre, the liquid began to take shape, frothing and bubbling up into the form of the hideous black spirit.

Miss Thomson put her hands to her mouth to stifle a scream. Her body froze as she saw the orange-haired boy step from behind the moving tentacles of the spirit. She drew on every ounce of her courage to open her lips and call out to Ryan. "Ryan, stay back from it! Don't go any closer!" she cried out.

Ryan looked over at Miss Thomson, but his eyes were glazed and trance-like; his expression empty.

Jack Ridley turned towards Miss Thomson and grinned as his hand reached out to Ryan for the coin.

"NO!" Miss Thomson screamed, weaving her way through the marshy ground. "Ryan, don't hand over the coin!"

She watched in horror as Ryan slowly raised his hand.

Chapter 8
The Connection

Miss Thomson had to do something. She picked up a stone. As Ryan touched Jack's fingers with the silver coin, Miss Thomson threw the stone with all her might. "Leave him alone, you monster!" she screamed.

The stone shot through the air and sailed through both Jack Ridley and the black spirit.

"No!" shouted Jack Ridley. "It's mine, give it to me."

Ryan opened his fingers and let the coin drop. Miss Thomson watched the glinting coin fall to the ground and disappear from sight. Jack's image weaved and distorted, his arms flailing, reaching out and grasping at thin air.

Suddenly Jack Ridley and the evil black spirit were gone.

Ravens screamed above. Then, within seconds, the wood became still and silent.

Miss Thomson looked around. Only two people remained standing in the glade – herself and Ryan. Relief swept over her. She had saved Ryan. She dashed up to him and grabbed his shoulders. He looked white and shaken but he was, thankfully, alive and well.

61

"The coin," he said quietly, "it's gone. It's finally gone back into the pond."

"Yes, Ryan," said Miss Thomson, her voice wavering, "it's all gone. We're safe now."

A few days later, everyone in class was waiting with anticipation for their research marks. Ryan had been given time off school to recover, and now Miss Thomson was looking forward to seeing him back to his usual self.

She stacked up the research papers and smiled at her pupils waiting to hear about their projects; everyone that is except Shane Lewis and Ryan Webb.

Much to Miss Thomson's surprise, Shane and Ryan sauntered into class fifteen minutes late. They had suddenly become the best of buddies.

"Sorry, Miss. Ryan lost his school bag and I had to help him find it," said Shane.

Miss Thomson looked at Ryan. He was still white and a little gaunt, and had a distant look in his eyes. "Is this true, Ryan?" said Miss Thomson concerned.

"Yes," Ryan replied coldly.

Miss Thomson was stunned by Ryan's lack of response to her. He seemed unfriendly, rude even. "Ryan, come here please," she said.

Ryan stomped up to her desk.

"Ryan, what happened to Pinocchio?" she whispered with a smile.

"His nose kept growing," said Ryan flatly.

"Yes? And?" Miss Thomson searched the boy's eyes for some recognition, but there was nothing there.

The corners of Ryan's mouth curled up into a strange grin. "Well, Miss Thomson, everyone knows the puppet came to life and found a soul."

Miss Thomson shivered. Ryan's bright blue eyes stared piercingly through her, without a flicker of emotion. "Go and sit down," Miss Thomson said curtly. She watched Ryan arrogantly saunter to his seat. Her body turned to ice as she asked herself the terrifying question, "Have I really saved Ryan Webb?"